Mentoring in Higher Education:

Best Practices Workbook
Second Edition

Dr. Marcia E. Canton
Dr. David P. James

Mentoring in Higher Education:
Best Practices Workbook

© 1999 Dr. Marcia E. Canton & Dr. David P. James

ISBN: 978-1-61170-059-6

Second Edition

To order additional books, go to:
www.cantonassociates.com
or call **1-650-355-0496**

Printed in the USA and UK on acid free paper.

Robertson Publishing™
59 North Santa Cruz Avenue
Los Gatos, California 95030 USA
www.RobertsonPublishing.com

~ Acknowledgement ~

We would like to acknowledge the support, time, guidance, and creative energy given to us as we pursued our goal of providing an informative, comprehensive, blueprint for establishing a mentoring program.

Special thanks to Jon and Alicia Robertson who kept us on task and assisted us in every detail as we completed this project. This book is dedicated to anyone who would like to assist another human being in realizing their dream.

"With ordinary talent and extraordinary perseverance, all things are attainable."
— Thomas Foxwell Buxton

Table of Contents

Preface

The *Mentoring in Higher Education: Best Practices Workbook* introduces basic mentoring concepts that should be mastered for success in mentoring program development and mentor/protégé relationships.

- **Part I** of the Workbook includes suggested exercises and questions which essentially follow the topic heading in the *Mentoring in Higher Education: Best Practices* book.

  Each suggested exercise or question begins with a list of skills or proposed mentoring activities that program administrators, mentors and protégés can use as additional sources of training or professional development activities. In all cases, the exercises and questions are specifically designed to enhance the mentoring process.

- **Part II** of the Workbook consists of seventeen protégé vignettes. The vignettes, with specific questions, are designed for activities and skills to be utilized by mentors in response to protégé's needs as depicted in the individual vignettes.

- **Part III** of the Workbook consists of faculty vignettes with suggested questions related to the qualities of each faculty candidate who wish to participate in the University Mentor Program. Based upon the individual profiles of the prospective faculty mentor candidates, this exercise is designed to determine whether the mentor qualifications are compatible for successful pairing with program protégés.

  This section concludes with "An E-mail Message to a Protégé." This sample e-mail serves as a mechanism for the reader's review and discussion of the scope of knowledge and resources a mentor is expected to have. It also demonstrates the effectiveness of mentoring even when the mentor and protégé are separated geographically.

- **Part IV** of the Workbook consists of basic questions for starting and implementing a mentoring program. This exercise is designed for mentor program coordinators and administrators to examine their present mentoring program. This exercise is also designed for administrators of mentor programs to develop a checklist in response to the questions presented for starting and implementing a mentoring program.

PART I

SUGGESTED EXERCISES/QUESTIONS AS SUPPLEMENT TO

Mentoring in Higher Education: Best Practices

Suggested Exercises/Questions

Item	Reference and Page Numbers	Suggested Exercises/Questions
1.	*Best Mentoring Practices in Academic Institutions* Page 3	Develop a checklist on the best practices you have developed in the formulation of your mentoring program. Determine what areas you need to further develop or strengthen in your present program. If you are in the process of developing a mentoring program, review the best practices recommended by Canton and James.
2.	*Retention and the Significance of Mentoring* Pages 4-5	Is your mentoring program designed to increase the retention of diverse student population? If so, do your workshops and activities for protégés and mentors relate the significance of your mentoring program to the issue of retention?
3.	*Definitions of a Mentor and Mentoring* Pages 6-7	Have both mentors and protégés respond to the definitions. See if they have additional definitions based upon their experiences as a mentor or as a result of having a mentor in their lives.
4.	*Progtégé's Definition of Mentoring* *Pages 7-8*	In your workshop of protégés, have them give their definitions or interpretation of mentoring based upon the examples. In addition, extend this exercise to your mentors and have them give their perception of mentoring based upon the alphabet M through G. You can also give both mentors and protégés a pre-test on the meaning of mentoring (M through G), and then give them a post-test upon conclusion of the academic year. Compare pre-test and post-test results to determine the increase in perception and knowledge of the mentoring process.
5.	*Diverse Roles of a Mentor* Page 9	Have your mentors share from their perspectives the diverse roles of a mentor that best fit their profile in your mentoring program.
6.	*Diverse Roles of Mentoring* Pages 9-10	Have your mentors check their top five diverse roles of mentoring or as many as they perceive at this time in the mentoring process.
7.	*Principles of Effective Mentoring* Pages 10-11	Have both mentors and protégés comment on the principles of effective mentoring. You may, in an exercise, have them prioritize their top five or tten at this time. Have both mentors and protégés explain their choices and why they chose their prioritized principles of effective mentoring at this point in the mentoring relationship.

8.	*Program Development: Program Planning* Pages 12-15	Meet with your planning staff or committee to initiate or highlight specific strategies in planning a mentoring program based upon the following: (a) the first steps; (b) institutional commitment; and (c) roles of faculty, staff and students in the planning and development of your mentoring program.
9.	*Essential Elements of a Planned Mentoring Program/Establishing the Mentoring Program* Pages 15-17	Develop a checklist or a self-evaluation. Determine what areas you need to further develop or strengthen your present mentoring program.
10.	*Mission Statement* Pages 17-18	Do you have a comprehensive mission statement for your program? If so, does it clearly highlight the purpose of the mentoring program.
11.	*Mentoring Program Goals and Objectives and Outcomes* Pages 18-19	Are your goals and objectives clearly defined? Are your goals and objectives linked to expected outcomes in your mentoring program? Have you clearly communicated your goals and objectives to participants in the program and appropriate officials within the institution and external community?
12.	*Pitfalls in Mentoring Programs* Page 20	Develop a checklist. Determine what areas you need to develop or improve upon to eliminate or reduce pitfalls in your mentoring program.
13.	*Screening, Selection and Training* Page 20	Review your eligibility criteria in screening and selecting your mentors. Describe the criteria you utilize in selecting mentors. Does your criteria coincide or differ from that recommended in *Best Practices*?
14.	*Checklist for Mentor Qualifications* Page 20	Do you have a checklist for mentor qualifications? Have your mentors utilize this exercise in listing their top five or ten in priority order. They can also list qualifications that are not shown in the recommended list.
15.	*Mentorship Application* Page 25	Have you developed an application for your potential mentors? If so, what specific information are you requesting on your present application?
16.	*Interview Questions for Potential Mentors* Page 26	Do you have specific interview questions for potential mentors? What is the role of the interview process in the selection of your mentors?
17.	*Mentoring/Protégé Matching* Pages 26-28	What are the major criteria you are utilizing or plan to utilize in the mentor/protégé matching process? Does it reflect the mission and goals of your program?
18.	*Training for Mentors and Protégés* Pages 28-30	What are your specific training activities for protégés and mentors? Are desired outcomes related to your overall mission and goals?
19.	*Strategies for Effective Mentoring* Pages 30-31	Provide your mentor with reminders or literature emphasizing effective mentoring strategies. In your meeting(s) with mentors, have them share effective strategies with one another.

20.	*Roles and Responsibilities of Mentors* Pages 31-32	Do you have specific roles and responsibilities for your mentors? Have your mentors comment on their roles, responsibilities and strategies that best fit their profile and qualifications at this point in the mentoring relationship.
21.	*Mentor's Expectations* Page 33	What are your mentor's expectations? Have mentors discuss their expectations in establishing the mentoring relationship with assigned protégé.
22.	*Roles and Responsibilities of Protégés* Page 34	Do you have specific roles and responsibilities of protégés? Does your workshop activities for protégés emphasize their responsibilities in the mentoring program?
23.	*Mentoring Activities* Pages 35-36	Do you have carefully designed mentoring activities for your mentors and protégés?
24.	*Protégé Agreement* Pages 34-35	Mentors and protégés, in some instances, enter into agreements as part of the protégé/mentor relationship. Does your program need this kind of agreement? If so, why? If not, why?
25.	*Student Mentoring Program Status Report* Page 39	How do you monitor the academic progress of your protégé? Is there an agreement between the protégé and mentor regarding this significant aspect of the mentoring relationship?
26.	*Goal Setting and Action Planning* Pages 40-44	Have your mentors discuss with their protégés the significance of goal-setting activities. Have the mentors, in their initial activities, ask protégés about their academic and personal goals. Have the mentors discuss time tables and target dates for completion with the protégés. Have the protégés and mentors mutually decide upon objectives and goals for completion during the mentoring process and afterwards.
27.	*Stages in the Mentoring Relationship* Pages 45-48	Have both mentors and protégés comment on the mentoring relationship. Have them identify where they are in the mentoring relationship at this time and where they plan to go as the relationship continues.
28.	*Types of Mentor/Protégé Mentoring Relationships* Page 48	What are the types of mentoring relationships in your program that have developed between mentors and protégés?
29.	*Peer Mentors* Page 50	Do you have peer mentors or plan to utilize them in the future? What criteria have you established or plan to establish in the recruitment and hiring processes? Is the interview process a criteria for the hiring of your peer mentors? Do you have a position description for peer mentors?
30.	*Mentor Job Description* Pages 51-52	Do you have a position description for your mentors? Is it reflective of their mentoring responsibilities? Is it reflective of the mission and the goals of our program?
31.	*Project Director Job Description* Page 53	Does the project director have a written job description? Is your position widely known to participants in the mentoring program?

32.	*Mentoring on the Graduate Level* Page 54	There are statistics and recommendations related to mentor programs designed to enhance the persistence and retention of minority students in graduate school. Schedule training sessions with your mentors to alert them to the factors, mentoring functions, goals and strategies described in this segment.
33.	*Mentoring of Program Participants* Pages 55-56	Do you have a monitoring component of your mentoring program to determine to what extent the program is achieving its goals?
34.	*Protégé Outcomes, Protégé and Mentor Benefits, Institutional Outcomes* Pages 57-58	Be able to determine or identify benefits of your program (mentors, protégés, and institutional) through your input, monitoring and evaluation process.
35.	*Publicity Measures* Page 60	Do your present publicity measures clearly communicate the purpose, goals, and achievements of your mentoring program?
36.	*Program Evaluation* Pages 63-65	Review your criteria in receiving input from your protégés and mentors. Be sure that your evaluation instruments are designed to identify strengths and weaknesses of your program. Upon receiving evaluation input, begin proposing recommendations for change or modifications in your present program.
37.	*Program Evaluation Factors* Pages 64-65	Begin to answer the questions posed on "Factors Related to Evaluation of Mentoring Programs" to develop an evaluation plan for your mentoring program. List the variables that will be important to consider in your evaluation.
38.	*Program Evaluation Examples* Pages 67-72	Review the examples for evaluating Mentors, Protégés, and Advisory Board Members. Which terms are of particular relevance to your Mentor Program?
39.	*Conclusion* Page 73	Re-read our summary and conclusion. As a result of this book, what steps will you take to develop your mentor program? Or, what steps will you take to improve your mentor program? List at least three ideas you have gained from reading this book. What additional questions do you need to get answers for, prior to implementing your ideas?

PART II

PROTÉGÉ VIGNETTES

Questions to Answer about the Protégé

Directions: Please use these questions to serve as a guide in responding to each vignette.

1. List those characteristics you think are most important and revealing about the prospective protégé?

2. What assumptions do you think the prospective protégé is making about the Mentor Program?

3. What expectations do you think the prospective protégé has about participating in the program?

4. What are the mentor qualifications or personal qualifications you would utilize in assisting the prospective protégé?

5. If you were the Mentor of this protégé, what mentoring strategies or principles would you provide such as:
   - proposed roles and responsibilities of the protégé
   - mentor expectations
   - mentor and protégé initial activities
   - mentor/protégés program agreement
   - goal setting and action planning activities
   - anticipated outcomes

6. What evaluation strategy or strategies would you utilize to determine the success of the advice or guidance given to the protégé?

Amado P.

As a senior in high school, being the first in his family to even consider post-secondary education, Amado was "intimidated" by the idea of attending college. He didn't know if he would be prepared for such an intense educational environment; yet here he is today, a Dean's Scholar with the potential of entering a doctorate program at the university of his choice. Amado has extra-ordinarily high aspirations for himself as a professional and believes that the Mentor program can assist him in achieving these goals.

He plans to enter the field of Education and serve on the Board of Trustees for his state. Ultimately, he would like to make a significant impact on the standards and level of education that is received in the public school system. He would like to set the standards so that these students are prepared to successfully compete at the university level, beginning at the elementary-level of education. As a member of the Board of Trustees, Amado hopes to influence the high school and the middle school curriculum to meet the needs of the country's changing demographics, which includes an increase of the Latino population. He would also try to increase the graduation rate of "historically underrepresented groups" at the university level, which are predominantly Latinos and African-American students.

Amado recognizes that there are many steps to achieve this level of success within the educational field, including the successful completion of a Doctorate Degree in Education Administration. He feels the acquisition of a post-baccalaureate degree is not only important, but necessary for anyone who intends to accomplish these goals. He has recently developed high expectations of himself and is aware of the necessary requirements to achieve the goals he has set. However, though he has not acquired the skills to compete in a doctorate level program, Amado has the potential to enter and excel with the proper guidance and support. Upon entering the Mentor Program, Amado anticipates the consistent encouragement from peers, faculty and staff to complete his Bachelor's Degree and continue into a doctorate program. Not only does he expect to receive guidance, but also offer strength to his peers in order for them to reach their goals as well. The support will also broaden his knowledge about graduate requirements, various graduate programs and how to make the most of graduate studies. The guidance and leadership from everyone within the program will benefit Amado to successfully enter graduate school.

Amado feels very fortunate to have his mind focused on attaining a doctorate degree. He has the potential to succeed in a post-baccalaureate program and can assist others to excel beyond their own potential. He is very determined to improve not only his own educational status, but the status of others as well. The Mentor Program can challenge him with academic research that will establish the foundation necessary to make an impact on the educational system. He is looking forward to the challenges and opportunities the program has to offer. He understands the importance of competent research skills, especially in developing educational programs for school-age children. These are techniques and methods he feels he needs to develop along with the skills to write a cohesive research publication. If Amado were selected to participate in the Mentor Program, he could benefit tremendously from the experience of the Summer Research Project, along with presenting the research at various universities. He also anticipates receiving information from various graduate programs nationwide so he can choose the best program to help him reach his goals. He awaits the challenge the Mentor Program has to offer and learning from others as well.

Bertha M.

A strength of Bertha's in preparing for doctoral work is getting good grades, and keeping her grade point average up. Her inclination is toward higher learning. She keeps a positive mental attitude and hates idleness. She continues on, no matter how many obstacles confront her. Bertha's adage is "at no time, ever give up on your dreams". Bertha identifies one of her weaknesses as having no direction. Her goal is to reach work at the doctoral level. Bertha despises non-productivity. She decided to seek support from faculty. Another of her weaknesses is being a perfectionist.

Bertha's reason for wanting to undertake graduate study at the doctoral level is because she would be the first in her family to do so. Neither she nor her parents or anyone in her family ever had an opportunity for an education. She remembers her mother saying she had to walk nine miles to the schoolhouse and nine miles back growing up as a girl in Tennessee. Most of her time was spent in the cotton fields picking cotton. Since her mother didn't have a choice between going to the field to pick cotton or attending school to get an education, she didn't get a chance to attend school that often. Bertha never heard her mother say that she ever attended a school. Her parents didn't live together, and when she visited her father, he never mentioned that he'd ever gone to school. She had nowhere to study and was always chased from the table while trying to do so because her stepfather had to eat.

Bertha's folks lived on a plantation in Tennessee before coming north. Every morning, the wagon would come and they all got on the wagon and went to the field to pick cotton. The wagon would return at sundown. The opportunity for education wasn't there; they never had any aspirations for school. Her mom had six children and worked real hard at a Laundromat, while her grandmother made sure they were cared for and sent to school. Her father lived within walking distance with a woman who had twelve children. Two were her dad's. Bertha remembers, while in junior high school, begging him for lunch money, which he never gave her. She was always hungry as she watched her sister eat a hot lunch because she was under-weight. There was just no money for her, ever. Bertha would go outside at lunchtime, weather permitting so no one would notice she didn't have any lunch.

The junior high school was divided into sections one through twelve. Sections one and two were designated as those who would most likely succeed. Bertha was in section seven. She now knows these sections were a recipe for disaster. All of the poor kids were in the lower sections. Their parents didn't know how to fight for them in those days, they felt they had no rights and of course no education. High school was no better. African-Americans had to walk to high school, which was at least seven to eight miles one way. They cut a path through the forest for a short cut. There was no bussing in those days. Blacks couldn't participate in school clubs or any extra activities.

Bertha and her two sisters shared a room. They shared bunk beds and she had a full size bed. Her stepfather sold her bed with her mother's approval, and it was replaced with a roll-away-bed. Her grandmother made a mattress out of feathers for it. Bertha became pregnant at age 15, an emancipated minor at age 16; the baby came shortly after. Exactly one year and four days after the birth of her first child, her second baby was born at age 17.

Bertha wants to be in a position to address some of societies social ills, speaking with confidence and authority after having earned the credentials to do so. She plans to enter the field of research and do public speaking on her findings. Peers critiqued her in her speech class, as one who would make a great speaker some day. She has a dream that some day she will address millions.

Bertha feels she should be selected for participation in this program because given her background coming from a poor Black broken home, she should be a statistic or a prostitute. The lack of opportunity has been handed down as a legacy, and she would break the cycle in her family. She is from a background of object poverty, yet she's never grown bitter because she always had her dreams.

She expects to gain guidance from this experience. The assistance of a faculty mentor that will help her strengthen her academic skills. Being selected for participation in this program would certainly help her prepare for the realization of her dream. She also views this program as allowing her to apply for an opportunity to become educated, an opportunity which was unforeseeable to her parents.

She would like to use her degree as a credential in support of and advocacy on behalf of those whom have no voice; the low income, low resource, and no option groups. She believes she has a lot to offer to society. She is a volunteer domestic violence counselor. At this time she volunteers at least twenty hours a month to the crisis hotline. She has been a volunteer to help combat illiteracy. She feels the education especially at the doctoral level will enable her to serve the community more thoroughly.

Consuelo S.

Consuelo feels this program will afford her the opportunity to do extensive research on a topic relating to anthropology. The Mentor Program will also help her out financially when applying to graduate schools.

She is interested in expanding her knowledge in the field of anthropology, with an interest in the area of public policy, by someday working for a government agency or a worldwide organization in a cross-cultural setting. In applying her anthropological skills and background, she hopes to contribute solutions to the various "problems" that are emerging as a result of progress; for example, the realities of erroneous working conditions and/or environmental degradation prevalent in most developing nations.

Although the scope of progress (and its effects) is very generalized, Consuelo believes that the guidance of the Mentor Program will help her to narrow down her area of interest into something more specialized. She also thinks that attaining a doctorate in Applied Anthropology will not only allow her to be a part of the decision making process, but to influence it as well; thus, permitting her to employ or exercise her thinking skills to manage, evaluate, and interpret volumes of information on human behavior.

She proposes to sharpen and build on her existing transferable skills while in the Mentor Program. Such existing skills and abilities include: the ability to think critically, the ability to follow through on assignments, the willingness to accommodate to changing tasks and settings, the ability to work well with diverse groups of people, the ability to follow instructions, and the skill to translate and transcribe Spanish. There are certain transferable skills that she does need to develop, in which she believes the Mentor Program and the six-week summer course will aid in the process. Such skills to develop are: to formulate and articulate new concepts and ideas; to learn how to conduct ethnographies under the guidance of her mentor; to learn more about public policy; to gain knowledge in using new information technologies; and learn to access and apply this new information in her future career.

In the future, Consuelo desires to contribute to the world in a profound way. She believes that being a part of the public policy and decision-making process, even on a local scale, can give her the knowledge to make change on the international level. She believes that many small-scale cultures throughout the world are being exploited by powerful nation states as we speak. She sees it as her duty to help preserve what little is left of their ancestral lands and cultures. Many anthropologists and economists today believe that the processes of progress and development cannot be eliminated; examples being the tourist industry or the proliferation of multi-national corporations. She thinks that her responsibility as an anthropologist would be to act as an intermediary between nation-states and locals in the constant ethical disputes over land and resources, so that diplomatic negotiations may happen and the outcomes will benefit both parties involved.

Corina L.

For Corina, the most valued personal asset gained has been the confidence and adapted thought process culminated from extensive hands-on counseling while performing volunteer work for the Rape Crisis Center. When she began the Rape Crisis intervention work, she generally became nervous during the person's crisis calls. Since then Corina has managed to overcome this hurdle and now responds to Rape Crisis calls with the confidence and professionalism acquired only through experience, dedication, and the application of knowledge gained through an intensive study program. She now focuses on the patient with the support and information that is necessary to handle a crisis situation. Other related fieldwork includes working extensively with abused and neglected children, as well as the completion of a 40-hour certification program dealing with domestic violence. Although this fieldwork experience has been invaluable, she feels that she lacks knowledge about different types of graduate programs offered as well as which schools would be best suited to meet her specific area of concentration.

Corina is also in need of further education as to what types of programs are offered in Clinical Psychology and its related financial costs.

There are several reasons why Corina decided to pursue her education to the doctoral level. First, she hopes to teach at a University; therefore, it is essential that she receive a Ph.D. to qualify for a job of that stature. Attending graduate school will allow her the opportunity for intensive study in Clinical Psychology with the outcome being specialization in her field. Other goals include opening a private practice for low-income and minority groups and conducting research.

Corina has a good understanding of the issues surrounding those that come from lower socio-economic levels or from minority groups. Unfortunately, those that really need counseling services generally come from disadvantaged backgrounds and don't have the resources available to them to seek assistance. Those are the people she hopes to help.

The skill she has gained through working with the disadvantaged has prepared her for the future work that lies ahead. Corina is determined to reach her future goals, and knows she will utilize any skills and knowledge that she gains from the Mentor Program. She is detail oriented, hard-working, responsible, and passionate about undiscovered knowledge in the Social Sciences; therefore, she feels that working with a Mentor will be an exciting experience.

Graduate schools, programs offered, financial costs, and the application process is ladened with anxiety and confusion for Corina. She hopes through this program that her perspective will change and that she will leave with whatever requisite skills and information that she may need to attend a graduate school. Corina has taken research methods and feels comfortable performing library as well as lab research; however, she hopes to define these skills even further. Ultimately, through a teaching or counseling career, she wishes to return the emotional as well as intellectual body of knowledge imparted upon her by former teachers, back to the community. Through this program she hopes to gain a better understanding of the necessary skills that will be needed to attend the graduate school. She has had scholastic experience with research methods and lab research; however, she hopes to refine these skills even further. Lastly, Corina hopes that by being granted this opportunity, she will in turn be enabled to give opportunity to others.

Dana C.

D ana is in her sophomore year at the University. She is an EOP transfer student who returned to college as a full time mid-life re-entry student in 1993; exactly thirty years since her first year of college at the university had ended in academic and social probation. She graduated from a community college in 1996 with an AA degree in Liberal Studies. Graduation was bittersweet: while finishing her last semester at the community college, she was also sharing the last five months of her husband's life.

Returning to college in 1993 at the age of 49, her goal was to obtain an AA degree in Radiation Therapy. However, career placement testing convinced her to change her major to Occupational Therapy. Her new goal became transferring to the University; completing her major program and going on to obtain a Master's degree by the year 2001.

While working to complete her advanced general education courses, her EOP counselor introduced her to the Mentoring Program. It is now her desire to expand her minor and complete a Ph.D. program in Gerontology after earning her bachelor's degree in Occupational Therapy.

It is her theory that synergy gained from combining the disciplines of gerontology, hospice, and occupational therapy will improve patients' health and hence their lives during their end-of-life transition. Dana would like the opportunity to help educate others by preparing herself to teach at the university level.

Her personal experiences as a direct care giver and as the primary care giver with hospice, before her husband's illness and during his in-home hospice care, convinced her that improving and maintaining the healthy qualities of a person's life is the ethical responsibility of today's health care professional.

Participation in the Mentor Program would provide her with a mentorship in her chosen field of Gerontology and a network of fellow students. The confidence, grooming, and knowledge provided by a chosen scholar would be invaluable to her for she is working at an age when most people returning to college are working at a graduate level. It is her belief that the academic polish intellectual stimulation and motivation would make acceptance into graduate school a reality. The wise words of Adlai Stevenson and Robert Browning have danced through her head for many years: *"It is not the years in your life but the life in your years that counts; Grow old along with me! The best is yet to be."*

Eliza P.

Eliza's strengths of study have been tenacity, the desire to challenge her learning capabilities, and her enjoyment of the academic environment. At her present level of ability, she has utilized many classes to research autism and related disorders. Her writing skills are strong. She has spent many hours of her employment and volunteer time gaining a working knowledge of childhood developmental disabilities. Eliza believes that she has also had the advantage of gifted instructors who were generous with their time.

As for weaknesses, she has had to work for most of her academic career, only attending part-time. She is also the mother of two children with special needs who, until 1998, were below school age. Eliza is a visual learner who has extraordinary difficulty with math. She is hearing impaired and depends heavily on hearing aids. Since graduate study has always been a tentative goal for her, most of her education has been spent at the affordable community college level.

The reason Eliza is interested in study at the doctoral level is that such study is very detailed and in depth. Doctoral study offers a level of understanding not attainable at the baccalaureate level. There is also the tempting option of teaching.

Her career objective is to teach at the University while researching new diagnostic techniques and treatments for children stricken with developmental disabilities.

Eliza would like to be selected for this Program because she has enormous potential. She has first-hand and practical experience with autism and other related difficulties. She believes she could be a skilled researcher and diagnostician.

What she hopes to gain from the Mentor program is the luxury of studying full time, the opportunity to learn skills in research and applications and a chance to prove herself.

In return, the educational field would receive a competent associate and the psychological field would receive a practitioner with research as a integral part of her professional growth.

The community, always so generous to Eliza and her children, would receive a professional with first hand experience who also has diagnostic and educational capabilities. Eliza would then be in the unique position of demystifying and destigmatizing childhood developmental disorders to those she came in contact with. Eliza feels that these would be priceless abilities.

Elizabeth M.

Elizabeth is applying for the Mentor Program because she is interested in pursuing a Ph.D. in Psychology. She believes that this program will help her to become successful in obtaining her goals through research.

Obtaining a doctoral degree has been Elizabeth's lifelong dream. Through professional training she will gain the knowledge and ability necessary to understand, contribute to and influence changes in human conditions extending from the community to Washington D.C. Successful completion of a graduate program will increase her ability to perform well and add credibility. Additionally, she believes that modeling is an important factor in being able to inspire and persuade others that environmental restrictions can be overcome as long as individuals do not set limits on themselves.

Elizabeth is an African-American single-parent of two children, a non-traditional student as well as, a first generation college student. She is the only one out of six brothers and sisters to finish high school. Her mother received an 8th grade education and her father received a 4th grade education; both were laborers in the south. Her mother worked in domestic positions, farming, picking cotton, and various fruits. Her father was a logger and pallet-maker before moving into janitorial services. In the early years of their lives, her siblings were already working in the same employment as their parents.

Through the increases in opportunities, their lives changed, thus, the future outlook is better for their children and grandchildren. Counting her two children, a total of four out of thirteen children have graduated from high school thus far. Her grandchild is part of their third generation of children reaping the benefits of an educated, more informed and healthy environment. She has always operated on the premise that one person can make a difference and by endeavoring to succeed at all cost, the next generations might catch hold of the vision.

Elizabeth's experience occurred in the South during one of the most traumatic times in this Nation's history for African Americans. She experienced first hand the kind of prejudice, discrimination and racism that divided this Nation and continues to thrive. She knows, without a doubt, that when equal opportunities are denied, it stifles hope in the soul and creates despair. She knows what it means to be violated, beaten, spit on and treated like a criminal without provocation. She knows the evil of domestic violence and child abuse. She knows poverty and deprivation. Through hope, endurance and determination she fought her way through these difficult times. Mohandas K. Gandhi said, *"an eye for an eye will make the whole world blind."* It is this kind of thinking, courage, and strength that comes out of adversity to create a survivor's deep desire to make the world a better place for all. Paraphrasing the words of Elie Wiesel, Elizabeth states that we owe it to the world to remember our mistakes, and learn from them so that we never repeat them again. In this way we are triumphant. As a minority woman, adversity has made her strong and through these diverse experiences, she believes that she would make a great candidate for the Mentor Program, and she will contribute greatly to the field of psychology. Elizabeth believes that there are no greater problems than the social dilemmas we create.

In addition to her personal experience, Elizabeth has benefitted directly from numerous opportunities that came out of the Civil Rights Movements, and the Feminist Movements, as well as, the instruction and wisdom of many teachers, through religion, and literature. And looking back at the America that the Farmers dreamed, it is the same America that Langston Hughes spoke of in the following stanzas from "Let America Be Again."

> *"Let America be the dream the dreamers dreamed –*
> *…0, let America be Again –*
> *The land that never has been yet –*
> *…And yet / swear this oath*
> *America will be!"*

The contributions from individuals like Dr. Martin Luther King, Jr. with his "I Had A Dream" speech, or Sojourner Truth's "Ain't I A Woman," Harriet Beecher Stowe's "Uncle Tom's Cabin," and countless other historical figures have brought us this far. Elizabeth feels a personal responsibility and a moral obligation to all the forerunners for what they have done to secure a brighter future or America and the World.

Striving for excellence and making a contribution to the welfare of others is the best way that Elizabeth feels she can honor the forerunners, and excellence is required for success. She is challenged to create a stronger support network for her graduate success, and she believes that this program will provide that for her through guidance, graduate preparation, and opportunities to participate and work with others in the field of research.

Elizabeth is passionate about the disciplines of Social and Cognitive Psychology, and in particular areas regarding how we think, communicate, make decisions, interpret data, and interrelate, as well as, studying preconception and motivation. She believes that these studies would provide the most information toward working to empower individuals rather than continuing to create environments of prolonged dependence. She realizes that changes to our social structures are extremely difficult and resistant, and that the sustenance of solutions is affected by internal and external influences over time. Nothing is permanent and there are no guarantees. Be that as it may, she is an optimist and she believes in possibilities beyond the point where many may end their search, the quality of life is that important.

Through research, Elizabeth states that she may end up with more questions than solutions, but ultimately these questions will provide a place where she can learn to manipulate, and evaluate important data leading to important developments in understanding and thus to possible solutions. A significant number of minorities and women must be included in future scientific studies both on research teams and in the studies themselves; their input is pertinent to the balance and accuracy of the studies.

Fernando D.

The Mentor Program will give Fernando the tools to enter a graduate program in Ethnic Studies. His highest priority is earning a Ph.D. in this field. He will sacrifice many things in order to attain his goal. As a professor, his goal will be to present the views of poor people who do not have the opportunity to advance in positions of influence and power in this society.

Fernando feels that poor ethnic groups do not have equal representation in the decision-making process of this society. The unequal representation is very harmful to these minorities. For example, all decisions made through the political sphere affects everyone in this society. Therefore, minorities are at a disadvantage because they lack representation in these political decisions.

Most of his life, he struggled through school. Financially, he could not even dream of a higher education. He came from a family of six people. None of his family members graduated from a university. Throughout grade school he could not participate in many school activities. He spent most of his time working and helping his parents financially. He remembers a time when his father said that an education was not important. He would say that they would be more productive if they gave up and worked full-time. The only reason that they did not quit grade school was his mother. Their mother knew the importance of an education. His mother did not want her children breaking their backs with minimum wage labor.

Fernando's mother is the most influential person in his life. Hard work and commitment was what his mother has taught him. He does not know anybody as courageous and strong as his mother. She is his role model that has kept him away from trouble and motivated him to continue his education. Nobody in the world can compare with his mother.

Fernando is awaiting your decision.

Juan B.

Juan is a 32-year-old re-entry Chicano student who just completed his first year at the University with a cumulative GPA of 3.2. He is currently a senior, majoring in Behavioral Science-Sociology with a minor in Mexican-American Studies. He decided on this major because he wanted to learn about the indigenous peoples and how they were effected by the dominant culture. He is also interested in the reasoning, and state of mind that the dominant societies have on these smaller groups.

After graduating from high school in a migrant farm workers setting, Juan lived from paycheck to paycheck. He became frustrated at the dead end jobs and the lack of opportunities a person with no education has in this day and age. He enrolled at a community college in the fall of 1993 and graduated in the Spring of 1997. When he obtains his BA, his desire is to attend graduate school in Social Work. He is looking to work as a school career counselor at the college level to try and help other disadvantaged youths that are being left behind.

Juan laments that he did not have the proper guidance at the high school level. He was an unmotivated student who drifted through school day by day with no thought of the future at all. He even had problems enrolling at the community college level because a counselor felt he wasn't capable of reaching a certain level of math. It wasn't until he found a counselor he could relate to and communicate with, that he was able to straighten his enrollment out.

The research skills he has acquired since enrolling in college is using the Microfiche on-line searches for periodicals for term papers, interviews, and ethnographic research. He has also had informational tours of the library at the community college level as well as the university level. His hope is to strengthen his research and writing skills, and more importantly, his communication skills. He wants to experience, first hand, the hard work, dedication, and the intense research work that will be necessary in order for him to succeed at the doctoral level.

Juan's overall goal is to help underprivileged and disadvantaged minority youths who haven't had the opportunity to follow that dream. A particular research subject that would interest him is to determine the reasons why Chicano youths stray away or fail to graduate at the high school level. It is important to look at this trend from the viewpoint of the Chicano, and not from the dominant cultures point of view. And finally, why these individuals do not see education in their futures.

King Ming C.

Five years ago, King Ming came to the United States from Asia with her family. At that time, none of them spoke any English. This was one of the biggest obstacles in her academic and social life. She felt very frustrated because of her inability to communicate with her classmates, let alone understand what was going on in the classroom. However, during her two years at High School in New York, she was able to complete all of her English classes (from ESL 1 to English 8, which normally takes 7 or 8 years). She feels she has successfully overcome the language problem and has gained a reasonable command of the English language.

King Ming gained confidence in her ability to learn. She always wanted to be number one and believes that only by becoming number one could she prove that she has done her best. Once she sets a goal, she will devote all of her time and energy to accomplish the task.

King Ming cannot ignore the fact that everyone has his or her own weaknesses; she is no exception. She has been facing many difficulties in choosing her career goal. She likes to travel, likes sports, tennis, badminton, baseball, basketball and table tennis. Similarly she is interested in different careers: engineering and business. Perhaps one of her biggest weaknesses is wanting to learn as much as possible. She feels she has not done her best in everything.

When her parents were in China during the 60's, the time of the Cultural Revolution, they lost the opportunity to go to school. They have always regretted the fact that they did not have "enough" education. As a result, they have encouraged and instilled in her and her brother the desire to get the highest degree possible and to learn as much as possible. Therefore, working towards a doctoral degree is a primary goal in her life.

King Ming believes what she will gain from this experience will ultimately benefit the community of man. Engineering means building things. Society needs innovations and improvements. Engineers are trained to take care of these needs.

All one needs to do is look at the technological advances of the last decade and the dramatic changes in society—it all came about because of engineers! As an engineer, she hopes to assume this mantle of responsibility to better society and the livelihood of man.

Lidia A.

Lidia comes from a low-income Mexican family. In her family there are six children: three girls and three boys. Her oldest brother also went to college, graduating in 1996 as a chemical engineer. Her second to the oldest brother is still attending college and he will be graduating this spring. Of the girls, Lydia is the only one attending school at this time.

She is currently enrolled in the Environmental Studies Teaching Program. She plans to graduate in June 2001, with a BA in the Environmental Studies Teaching Program. At this moment Lidia feels that she needs more preparation for graduate school. Although she has a 3.67 GPA, she could use as much help as possible to help her progress in her studies. She feels that she needs a little more help in her writing skills. She still finds it difficult to write perfect English, since it is her second language, but she knows that with some help and practice she will improve her writing skills. She would also like to participate in the Summer Research Program because she thinks that by participating she will learn many new things.

Lidia's ultimate goal in life is to go to graduate school for administration. Her wish is to someday become principal of an elementary school. She believes that in the future, most of America will be made up of different minority groups. As it is, there are many minority groups at this moment all over America, but there is also a lack of minority educators in the public school system. She feels that going to graduate school and receiving her doctorate degree will help her achieve her goal. By getting her graduate degree, Lidia will have the qualifications that are needed to become a principal. She will do her best and try to help out the minority kids and teenagers. She feels that getting her doctorate degree will put her in a well-established position in which she will be able to help minorities.

In conclusion, Lidia is very thankful to have the opportunity to compete and to participate in a program like the Mentor Program, that helps minorities succeed in life and overcome all the prejudice in this society. If she gets selected to participate in this program, she will try to do her best and work very hard to achieve her doctorate degree. Lidia promises to take advantage of this wonderful program to help her become someone in life, to have an education and to be able to help others.

Margaret L.

Margaret's career objective is to eventually become the executive director of a women's resource center. She has seen so many women not live up to their full capabilities due to situations that they feel are insurmountable. These situations may stem from economic hardships, problems with self-esteem and or domestic abuse. She would like for women, especially those who are of ethnic descent, to feel that there are positive avenues that lead to solutions to these type of problems.

Margaret feels a special commitment to the women of her community because often times they do not seek assistance. Most of the time, they feel that no one will want to help them and that another "door will be slammed in their face." She would like to be a positive role model, a leader and to some, the key that opens the door that they once believed was not available to them.

A resource center that provides workshops, support group meetings and legal referrals would be beneficial to the type of women mentioned above and their children. Margaret believes one of her greatest strengths is determination. She has been in pursuit of her bachelor's degree for several years. Along the way she has encountered many obstacles. Some of which she thought she would never overcome; others, which have appeared to make her much stronger and wiser. She has always believed that education is the key to success and opportunity and has discovered that her future endeavors will need to be supported by higher levels of education.

Margaret is determined to finish the studies required to achieve a bachelor's degree in Health Science. Her intentions are to continue on in graduate school for a master's degree in Public Health. Not only would completing both of these educational goals be a major accomplishment for her, but would also instill in her a sense of self-confidence, which at times through this whole process has been lacking.

Being a single parent of two small children, Margaret would like to set an example to them by stressing the importance of education. At the same time, she would like to maintain a career in which she would be able to provide for them financially and be there for them physically as well. In this she means that she will have to acquire a job with an income that would suffice her working part-time and raising a family. She feels that in being a single parent she has deprived her children of the life that is so often deemed "normal". She feels like she owes it to them to go the "extra mile" to achieve the best for the three of them.

She believes that she is prepared for the graduate studies because she has seen the benefits and advantages that having a master's degree can promote. At this time she has the moral support that is needed to assist her along this challenging journey. A supportive family network and co-workers who are constantly pushing her to be all that she can be, make this opportunity a truly beneficial one for her.

Margaret is anxious to begin the Mentor Program.

Maria G.

Maria G. is the first in her family to attend college. She was born in Nicaragua, the seventh child of her family. When she was only three years old her family moved to the United States. She has only vague memories of her life in Nicaragua, but remembers her Father telling her that they were coming to America to seek a "better life."

Maria became interested in college when she attended a Science Fair at her Bible School Summer Program. She was fascinated with the wonders of science and began to ask questions of her teachers. She remembers vividly her high school Chemistry teacher's remark: "You will not do well in Science because your race is not good in this."

That was all Maria needed to impel her to exceed. She graduated from high school with honors and is now attending a Community College. It is the end of the first semester and she has received a failing grade in her Chemistry class. This, along with other problems, places Maria on probation. An "F" in Chemistry would result in having her dropped from the college. Maria went to her Chemistry professor asking to receive a "C" or "D" in the course.

She believed that she knew the material even though she did badly on both exams. The Chemistry professor refused to change the grade unless Maria had a legitimate excuse.

Maria, at first, refused to participate in the Mentoring Program because it would possibly demonstrate her inability to do college work. However, she now has second thoughts about the Mentoring Program and has applied for participation.

Maria M.

Maria M. was born in the United States, but both of her parents are from a small town in Mexico. When she was six years old her parents decided to return to Mexico. They believed that it was important for her to learn about her culture; a mission, which she feels, they have accomplished. When she was fifteen years old, her parents returned to the United States. After all, the family's economic stability was dependent on the packing company where they were employed. A cannery that Maria feels literally stole twenty years of her parent's lives.

Her parents did not have an opportunity to receive an education. They both had to leave school at a very young age to work in order to help raise the family. The third born in her family, Maria was the first one to receive a college education. Little by little the star she has always dreamed to reach seemed closer. Her parents did not have a chance to reach their star. It is her responsibility to reach her star and share it not only with them, but with her community.

Maria has faced many obstacles throughout her education, but she has always worked hard to overcome them. The first obstacle that she faced when she returned from Mexico was trying to learn a language that she did not understand. It was very frustrating, but with patience and courage she overcame that barrier. It was not easy, but she also knew that it was possible. She learned an important lesson, one has to work really hard in order to accomplish goals. She was very proud of herself, although there is one step that she regrets not taking while in school. She believes that she did not fight hard enough for her student rights.

She was never challenged in her classes. She always found herself in ceramic and cooking classes. The counselors never encouraged her to take physics or chemistry. No one told her what it actually took to become a scientist. Due to these circumstances, she ended up starting her college education not being well prepared. She had to spend a year taking classes that would prepare her for physics and chemistry. She lamented that some counselors just do not want to see what they call "Minority Groups" succeed in the education system.

Her career objectives are to earn a Ph.D. in Biology. By earning a Ph.D., she might be able to find a cure for a particular disease. At the same time, she will be able to extend a hand to help her people, just like the Mentoring Program is extending a hand to her.

Maria is interested in teaching at the college level since she believes that there is a demand for professors from minority communities (especially in the Science field). Throughout her education at the University, she has only had three professors of color.

Only one of whom is in the Sciences. While her other professors were helpful, she believes that school would have had a greater impact on her had she had more minority professors in the sciences.

Maria considers her education to be like a puzzle, in which there is a very important piece missing. The piece of the puzzle missing for her is research experience. It is her hope that the Mentoring Program will complete this missing piece.

Michelle H.

Abandoned by her alcoholic father, a Korean War Veteran, her mother tried to make a home for them in the United States. Without formal skills, her mother worked as a waitress, the only profession she had learned as a young girl in New York. Refusing to accept help from the public welfare system (and fearful she would be deported), she and Michelle lived in the most impoverished areas of towns — what Michelle would later come to know as a Ghetto.

When Michelle reached thirteen, her mother could no longer handle many of life's challenges, especially a mule-headed teenager. So packing her bags, she asked Michelle to leave. Mother Nature had been flighty in allowing Michelle to finish puberty by nine years of age; so getting a job and renting a room at thirteen was not an impossibility, especially when she could pass for eighteen. Although she was an honor roll student at the time, she could not maintain her 3.85 GPA while worrying about daily survival. The shame attached to the titles she wore: poor white trash, homeless teenager, high school drop-out, and eventually teenage mother, provoked her to develop skills and talents on her own. If the dream of becoming what she knew she could be was not enough, disproving her father's words after their thirteenth reunion, "You're a disgrace and you'll never be nothing," was.

While trying to keep a roof over her head, food in her stomach, and clothes on her back, she worked nine hour shifts at night while her son slept, and studied for her GED. After completing the exam, she taught herself how to type (approximately 85 wpm), applied for a promotion as Administrative Assistant, and received it.

In 1995, Michelle was married. Their son was born in 1996, the year they decided she should finally fulfill her dream to obtain a college degree. In 1998, their second son was born; and in 1999 (trying one last time for a girl) their twin boys were born. Michelle learned to study anytime and anywhere.

Six months after the twins were born their world crashed. Her husband hemorrhaged and nearly died. Terminal liver disease was the diagnosis; hepatitis C was the cause. Being a diabetic and experiencing a large volume blood loss, liver transplantation was not an option. While hospitalized from January until March (1999), a successful hepatic portal shunt was inserted (this has a 5-10 year success rate before hemorrhaging occurs again). Michelle knew then that completing college was not merely the realization of a dream, but a dire necessity. Her husband, a police officer, was now permanently and medically disabled.

During the last four years Michelle experienced many losses: her husband's illness and permanent disability; her "adopted" mother's sudden death; her natural mother's heart disease and subsequent move into their home; and their four year old son's fight for life with viral encephalitis, which resulted in spinal cord and brain damage. Being the sole caretaker for her husband, mother, and six-year old son is as challenging as it gets. The encouragement, compassion and respect she has received from her professors and peers at the University has compelled her spirit to press on even when the body was unwilling.

Although she has completed a bachelor's degree in Creative Arts (English emphasis) with a minor in Biology, Michelle's dream is to continue through a Master's Degree and then on to a Ph.D. She has two reasons for seeking this route. First to ready herself for doctorate studies by building a foundation of knowledge and honoring research skills in the field of immunology, under the close direction of a faculty member at the University. Second, to achieve a Ph.D. which would allow her to teach, encourage, and mentor other students to strive for excellence in education, especially those who have walked similar paths to her own.

Receiving acceptance into the Mentor Program will be the affirmation, guidance, and encouragement needed to complete the next two years of intense graduate work. Success in any field of study, especially when one comes from a disadvantaged socioeconomic background requires assistance and mentorship from those who have already walked through the graduate studies process. Although she may not be able to leave a wealth of material possessions for her five sons, she can leave them a legacy of honor; teaching them that to sacrifice the immediate for the long-range goal of higher education is by far the wisest choice.

Tony W.

Tony is an Asian-American student who was born in the United States six months after his family immigrated from Viet Nam. He is the second child in the family with an older brother and a younger sister. Both his brother and his sister work full time in the family business. Tony has always done well in school and until now, has managed to work in his family's restaurant business and attend college.

Tony is a sophomore majoring in "Computer Science." He has made an agreement with his parents that he will continue to assist them in their family business if they will allow him to continue in school. Tony works forty hours per week in his family's business and is finding that he needs more time for his studies.

Tony decided that he would like to work with a Mentor to figure out his career options. He was matched with a Mentor and they met only twice. Although, Tony would like to continue to participate in the Mentor Program, he does not have the time to meet with his Mentor or to participate in any of the activities. Tony's Mentor sees great promise in Tony and is concerned that his grades will begin to fail if he does not cut down on his work at the restaurant. Tony cannot break the commitment he made to his Father.

Yolanda W.

Yolanda is an African-American who was raised by her Mother. She is the oldest of four children and as a result, was called upon by her Mother to take care of her younger siblings. Yolanda also worked hard outside of the home to help support her Mother financially.

It has always been Yolanda's desire to be a Registered Nurse. She has been taking courses at the Community College and managed to get passing grades. Yolanda is now a sophomore at a four year college and is attending school full time in spite of her Mother's protest. Her Mother thinks that she should forget this "pipe dream" and get a successful job as a single parent raising four children. They have never gone hungry and have always had a roof over his heads. Yolanda should be grateful and should demonstrate that gratefulness by continuing to help her Mother.

Yolanda has had a hard time studying at home because her Mother leaves her with her sisters and brother while she works in the evening. She has difficult time studying at College because she must go home after her classes to take care of the children. Yolanda is not doing well in her courses now and is beginning to believe that her Mother is right.

PART III

FACULTY MENTOR VIGNETTES

Questions to Answer about the Faculty Mentor Vignettes

Directions: Please use these questions to serve as a guide in responding to each vignette.

1. List those characteristics you think are most important and revealing about the prospective mentor.

2. What assumptions do you think the prospective mentor is making about the protégés?

3. What expectations do you think the prospective mentor has about participating in the program?

4. As the Program Coordinator for selecting and pairing mentors with potential protégés, what mentor qualifications do you find in the resume summaries of Jerry Kamp, Rhonda Smith, and Mark Phelps?

5. Are the resume summaries compatible with the mission, goals, objectives and expectations of your mentoring program?

6. If you were the Program Coordinator, would you select this prospective mentor to participate? (Yes) (No)

   If Yes, why?

   If No, why not?

   What reasons would you give to the nonselected mentor?

Jerry Kamp

Jerry Kamp is an Associate Professor in the School of Business. He is a new faculty member at the university and is interested in engaging in activities which will give him recognition and ultimately promotion. He is anxious to participate in the Faculty Mentor Program for student-protégés because he sees it as a means for becoming visible to campus administration.

Jerry has much to offer his protégés and is even willing to set up computer classes for them. Although he is extremely busy, he is willing to fit his protégés into his tight schedule.

Mark Phelps

Mark Phelps is a Full Professor in Philosophy Department. He is interested in working with the Faculty Mentor Program for university students so he can get a better understanding of ghetto life among his protégés. This is a new area of interest to Mark and he is quite excited about this subject matter. In fact, he would like to set up some times when he can visit his protégés in their homes.

Mark says he is willing to expose his protégés to the cultural aspects of life they have missed, such as operas and plays. He wants 10 protégés assigned to him and is eager to get started.

Rhonda Smith

Rhonda Smith is an Assistant Professor in the Anthropology Department. She says she is excited about working with the Faculty Mentor Program for university students after spending one year abroad as a Peace Corps volunteer working with third world people. She is particularly interested in working with Hispanic students to get more exposure to this cultural group at this time.

Rhonda has provided you, the Program Coordinator, with her office hours and has indicated that she can only be available to her protégés at that time. She looks forward to participating in the program.

Questions to Answer about an E-mail Message to a Protégé

Directions: *Please use these questions to serve as a guide in responding to an e-mail message to a Protégé.*

1. List those characteristics you think are most important and revealing about this mentor.

2. What assumptions do you think the prospective mentor is making about the protégé?

3. What expectations do you think the prospective mentor has for the protégé?

4. What strategies have the mentor outlined for the protégé that would be useful for initiating a mentor/protégé relationship?

Anita,

First of all, congratulations on the deferral from Stanford. Now you have a very visible goal to work towards. Two things to emphasize for what will very likely be a busy year — say "NO" to everything that does not involve MA course work or research (volunteer stuff, sorority events, helping tutor struggling students). Although some of these things in parentheses may seem like the honorable and helpful thing to do, you must think like an individual if you really want to get out in a year. So, you are allowed to think of yourself and only yourself. Just say NO!!

The second thing is that you have to find someone on campus who will sit down with you and work out a concrete, reasonable plan for your time. I do not think that I am the most appropriate person given the distance and not having current knowledge about courses offered, etc. I can give you general advice, like what to spend the most time on, how to not emphasize all A's, etc. But you need an ally on campus. Try _____ or _____ (specific names provided).

Let me propose an approach for the Mentor Program. I think this would be most useful in getting you ready to propose your masters thesis. Contrary to popular belief, you can begin and finish a thesis in a year or so if you carefully plan and use your time wisely. What happens with the MA students on campus is that they work full time, take classes, and try to finish their MA degree. If you don't work, the only (ha,ha) things left are courses and research. So, if we can use the next 2 months as a planning and proposal session for your masters thesis research so that you can start it first thing in the fall, that would be the best use of your time.

I am very glad that you have found the references helpful. I think what I would like to see before we go any further are 3 lists of things. Here are the specifics:

List 1: A list of terms (not definitions, just terms) that you are comfortable with (and be conservative with "comfortable") with respect to research methods, stats, and the lingo.

List 2: A list of terms that you are NOT comfortable with (be liberal) with respect to methods, stats, and that lingo. List 1 and 2 should be as exhaustive as you can make them.

List 3: A 1 or 2 line description of research topics/ideas you would realistically like to pursue as a Masters thesis. Here is an example of a description: The effect of teacher presentation (strict or lax) on student participation and grades.

This description is not what I would want to pursue, but it is like a title for a journal article, it names variables and levels. It could be more specific; in fact, it should be for your purposes. I want this list to be ideas you want to work on, not what I would like to work on or anyone else for that matter. If you are going to get out of the program in a year, you have to be motivated to work on the research and it have to be something you can handle. Taking on a project specified by a faculty member may be okay if you are motivated by it, but those projects tend to proceed slower.

If you should decide to hang in there with me, I need to get some information to you from the Mentor Program. If you have a fax number, I could fax it to you. I am happy to work with you through the summer to help you get started on your thesis proposal. I will read any material you give me. I cannot (rules of the department) chair your thesis committee. I can be a reader, but you have to find 2 others on campus to be on your committee. For that purpose, I would rather that you not work on any of my "research" per se. If it is experimental, I will help. I do not think you should work on my research because I really need to be there in person to monitor progress. I would rather just be involved in planning, reading, and other input. So again, you need to find someone on campus who would be willing to work with you and really give you support to finish in a year like you want.

So, send me those three lists by next Monday (a week from today) — this is your "deadline". Send me the information on the Mentor program or send an email address for someone I can talk to within the program. I am trying to check email every other day or so. I will let you know when I have an office phone so we might be able to chat in real time.

Take care Anita, I will talk to you soon.

Your Mentor

PART IV

STARTING AND IMPLEMENTING A MENTORING PROGRAM

Basic Questions for Starting and Implementing a Mentoring Program

1. Why is the program needed? Who is the program intended to help (which target group)? What purposes will it promote? What needs will be fulfilled? How will you document the need for the pilot program — what evidence can you present?

2. How will objections (if any) from those not included in the pilot program be handled?

3. Who supports the program? How will support be gotten from others (at the top, middle, and grass roots levels)? What organizational politics must be taken into account — how?

4. Are existing organizational policies, structures, employee support services, mission, culture, etc., compatible with the concept of mentoring as a people development process that takes time to produce major results? If not, what will be done?

5. What concerns and expectations do participants have? Do others have? How will concerns be resolved? How will expectations be met?

6. What general program components are essential? Is a multicultural component needed? Why? Who will help you design, develop, implement these components? Is there a Mentoring Committee or Task Force to do these things? How will you get good representation on it?

7. How will you get input from potential participants and others so they "own" the program?

8. How will you orient prospective participants so the right people volunteer (who know what the program entails)?

9. How will mentors and protégés be finally selected (criteria, procedure, time frame, etc.)?

10. How will mentor-protégé matches be done? Will this be 1:1 or some other ratio?

11. What training do mentors and protégés need (content, methods, length, at what points

in time)? Why? Will training be contracted out? Or done internally? Or a mixture? What are the benefits of each approach?

12. How will mentor and protégé commitment be motivated? Is mentoring an add-on to existing responsibilities or will time be allocated for mentoring to happen? What tangible organizational support needs to be provided?

13. How will withdrawal from the program be facilitated? (for mis-matches, not getting value from participating, not enough time, etc.)

14. Who will be the Program Coordinator? Will time be specially allocated for this responsibility—or is this an add-on? What training does the Coordinator need to run the program and monitor the mentoring process to increase success?

15. How will the organization ensure that mutual benefits result—for protégés, mentors, and the organization?

16. What will happen if the pilot is not as successful as expected—will it be discontinued? Modified and tried again? Or another prototype tried?

17. How will program effectiveness in meeting intended goals be determined?

18. What strategies will be used to improve program components based upon input from participants in the mentoring program?

Conclusion

The challenge of developing successful mentoring programs is not an easy task. It requires leadership by those in the position of authority to ensure that mentors, protégés, and supportive cast understand the role of mentoring and the positive implications of successful mentoring programs.

The exercises and professional development activities suggested and recommended in this Workbook were designed to enhance not only program development, but also the successful pairing of mentor/protégé relationships.

Finally, this Workbook and proposed activities were designed to generate actions in the mentoring process and consequently influence positive mentoring outcomes. Best wishes.

Dr. Marcia E. Canton

Marcia E. Canton, Ph.D., is an educator and consultant, specializing in organization and management development. She is President of Canton Associates, a consulting firm developed to improve the effectiveness of educational institutions and the workplace by assisting decision makers and managers in a diverse labor force. Dr. Canton is a Professor Emeriti from San Jose State University where she taught a myriad of health, diversity and management courses more than twenty-five years. She also served as the first Coordinator of the Faculty Mentor Program which received a Chancellor's award for outstanding service.

Dr. Canton conducts research on the effects of educational support programs (such as mentoring) on first generation, low income, minority students.

As a member of the Board of the International Mentoring Association, she and Dr. David James conducted workshops on developing and evaluating successful mentor programs. They also conducted workshops for students only where they were able to provide encouragement and direction to college students. Dr. Canton was a member of the Board of the International Mentoring Association for 10 years.

She presently serves as an Academic Advisor at Holy Names University in Oakland, California where she is assisting in the development of a Mentor Program for baccalaureate nursing students. She is also a member of Third Age Task Force—an organization that supports nurses over 45 years of age in becoming mentors for new nurses. Dr. Canton continues to travel all over the country to speak on the importance of developing sound structural support for first generation students.

Dr. David P. James

Dr. David P. James is an educator and consultant specializing in leadership development for institutions and individuals who conduct or wish to develop mentoring programs. He is also President Emeritus of the International Mentoring Association, having served as President of the Association from 1989 – 2000.

Dr. James is internationally known as one of the leading experts in training, establishing, and evaluating mentoring programs. He served as the Project Director of the Prince George's Community College Black and Minority Student Retention Programs from 1988 – 1991. During this period, the retention programs with their formalized mentoring component of administrators, faculty, and staff, were cited in 1989 by U.S. News and World Report as being one of the nation's best for two year and community colleges. The retention/mentoring programs received the Award of Merit from the Maryland Association of Higher Education in 1990, and was also the recipient of a Program Retention Excellence Award from the Noel/Levitz Centers for Institutional Effectiveness, 1990.

In 1988, Dr. James was honored as the outstanding administrator at Prince George's Community College for his work in mentoring and student retention. In 1989, he was the recipient of an Individual Excellence Award from Noel/Levitz Centers for Institutional Effectiveness. In 2007, Dr. James received the President's Medal from Prince George's Community College, the highest award given to an employee of the college.

Dr. James retired in March 2008 as Dean of Educational Development and Degree/Extension Centers and Special Programs at Prince George's Community College, Largo, Maryland.

Contact Information

Dr. David P. James and Dr. Marcia E. Canton have been committed to the retention and graduation of students in higher education for over thirty years. They are available to conduct on-site workshops at your respective institutions of higher education.

Contact:

Dr. Marcia E. Canton
e-mail Dr. Canton: **drcanton@pacbell.net**
fax Dr. Canton: **(650) 355-0496**
www.CantonAssociates.com

Dr. David P. James
e-mail Dr. James: **drjames@dpjmentoring.com**
fax Dr. James: **(410) 997-0585**
www.DPJMentoring.com